FRO
2.0

Bellah

AZU's Dreams of Thailand
Bangkok
Published in 2005 by AZU Editions Ltd.
13/F, Silver Fortune Plaza
1 Wellington Street
Central, Hong Kong
www.azueditions.com

Produced by ink it Group Co. Ltd.
111 SKV Building, 3/F
Soi Sansabai, Sukhumvit Soi 36
Klongton, Klongtoey
Bangkok 10110, Thailand
Tel: 66 (0) 2661 2893
Fax: 66 (0) 2661 6895
info@inkitgroup.com
www.inkitgroup.com

ISBN 988-98140-3-X

Printed in Thailand

Copyright 2005 AZU Editions Ltd.

All rights reserved. No part of this publication may be reproduced, stored in a retrieval system or transmitted in any form by any means, electronic, mechanical, photocopying, recording or otherwise, without the prior written permission of AZU Editions Ltd. All content, text, illustrations and photographs in this publication are protected by national and international trademark and copyright laws. Any infringement of the rights of AZU Editions Ltd. may lead to prosecution without warning.

For information about reproduction rights to the photographs in this book, contact ink it Group Co. Ltd.

Sponsored by

Thai Airways International
Public Company Ltd.

Tourism Authority of
Thailand

AZU'S
DREAMS OF THAILAND

Bangkok

Photographs by Dave Lloyd
Text by John Hoskin

AZU

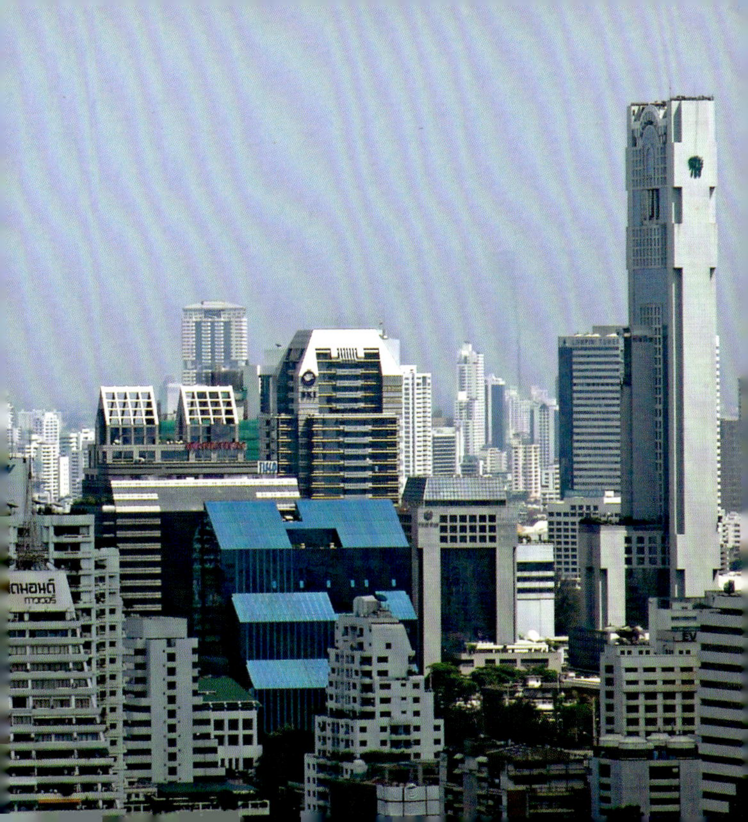

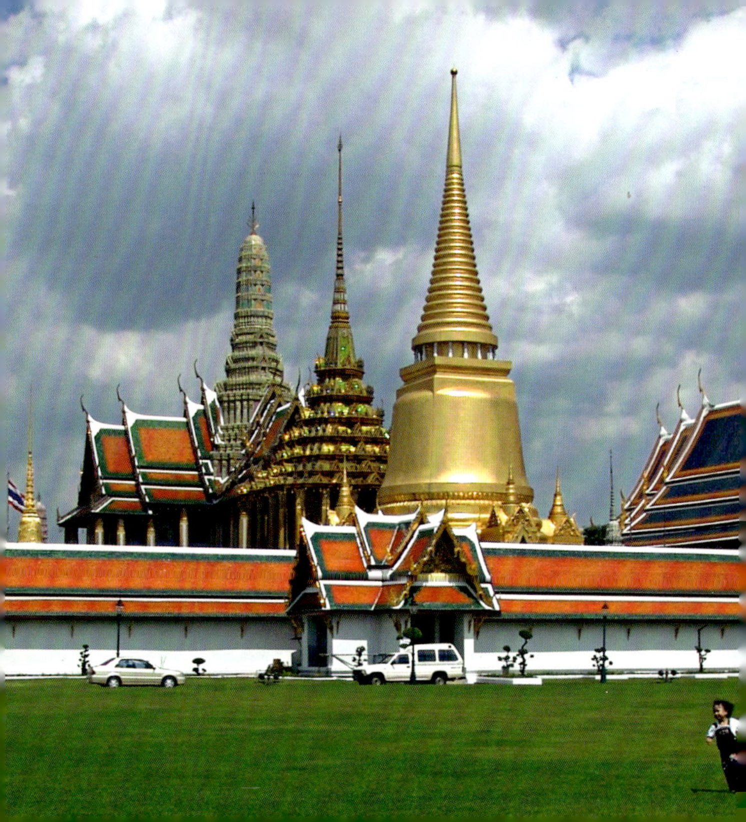

Golden spires
and orange-tiered roofs,

saffron-robed monks and serene Buddhas tell of Bangkok as an exotic city of temples and palaces. Yet equally it is a modern metropolis of office towers and condominiums, of concrete and glass-curtain walls, of business-suited executives and traffic-snarled streets.

Essentially a paradox, a seemingly impossible blend of old and new, Bangkok can be all things to all people. Here, in what the Thais call 'The City of Angels', are fulfilled dreams of both classic Oriental wonder and contemporary indulgence.

Bangkok was founded as the Thai capital in 1782 and, sited on the east bank of the Chao Phraya River, its early development followed an established riverine pattern. Royal and other major buildings were constructed facing the river. Beyond, a network of canals served as highways and byways into the larger urban area, hence the old soubriquet 'Venice of the East'.

Those days have long since vanished and most of the canals have been paved over to make way for the automobile. Then came expressways, flyovers, and elevated and subway train systems, while new buildings ever seek to rise above their neighbours. Amazingly, in the wake of massive modern development, Bangkok keeps its essence. It may in part echo Tokyo, Los Angeles or Chicago, but an immutable Thai style prevails so that

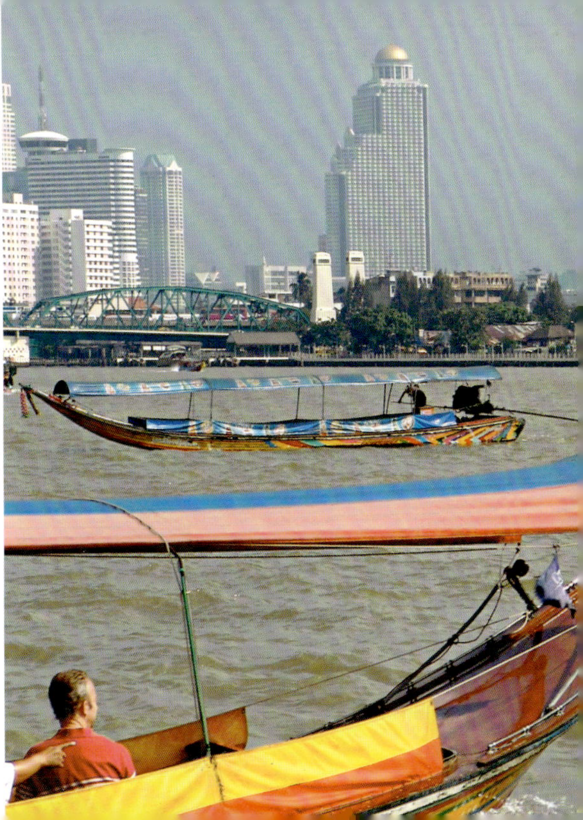

Bangkok remains inescapably Bangkok just as Gertrude Stein's rose is always a rose.

It is this 'Thainess' that, if not quite explaining the paradoxes, certainly makes them acceptable. Style extends beyond the obvious, whether in the grace of Thai classical dance or just in the simple wai greeting, and permeates the culture so that adopted foreign influences are always adapted into something specifically Thai.

British author Alec Waugh captured the essence of the city when he wrote, 'Bangkok has been loved because it is an expression of the Thais themselves, of their lightheartedness, their love of beauty, their reverence for tradition, their sense of freedom, their extravagance, their devotion to their creed — to characteristics that

are constant
and continuing
in themselves.'

Thus in spite
of a modern world
of dynamic change,
Bangkok manages to
preserve its cultural
heritage to a marked degree. In the soaring roofs
and gleaming spires of the Grand Palace and
the city's countless historic temples — Temple
of the Emerald Buddha, Temple of the Reclining
Buddha, Temple of Dawn and many other
evocative shrines — you are presented with
dazzling images of the Orient of old. And
contained within Bangkok's major monuments
and sights are treasures of the nation's artistic
and cultural endeavour that typify the land and
the people.

Nor are glimpses of the past found only in
the monumental; they are also seen in daily life,

where they add startling touches of colour and confound our conceptions of the contemporary and the ordinary. Files of saffron-robed monks making their early morning alms round, for instance, present a scene essentially unaltered by the passing of time. Today's backdrop of high-rise buildings only adds wonder to this and other traditional sights from which Bangkok continues to draw definition.

But if Bangkok keeps its heritage and clings to its traditions with pride and devotion, at the same time it embraces with a rare exuberance all that is new, fun and pleasurable. A host of world-class hotels welcome their guests to unsurpassed luxury; countless restaurants serve not only Thailand's spicy specialities but also virtually

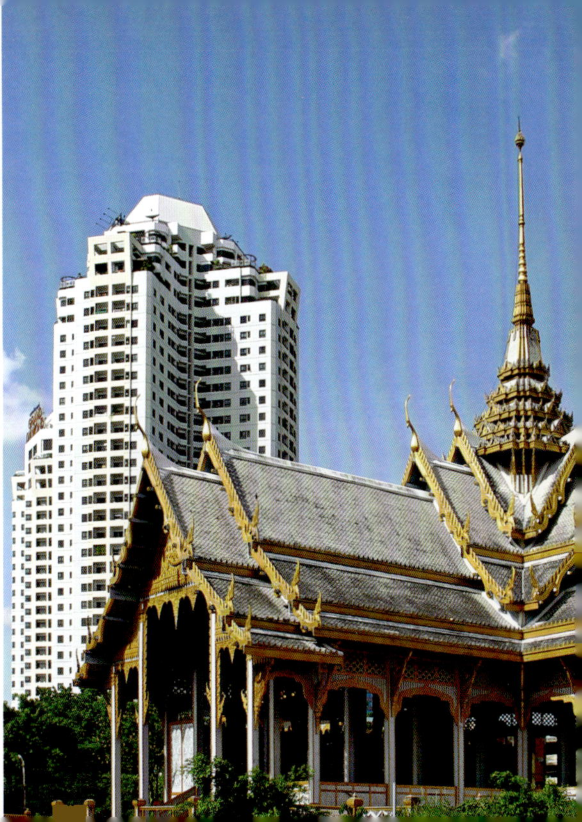

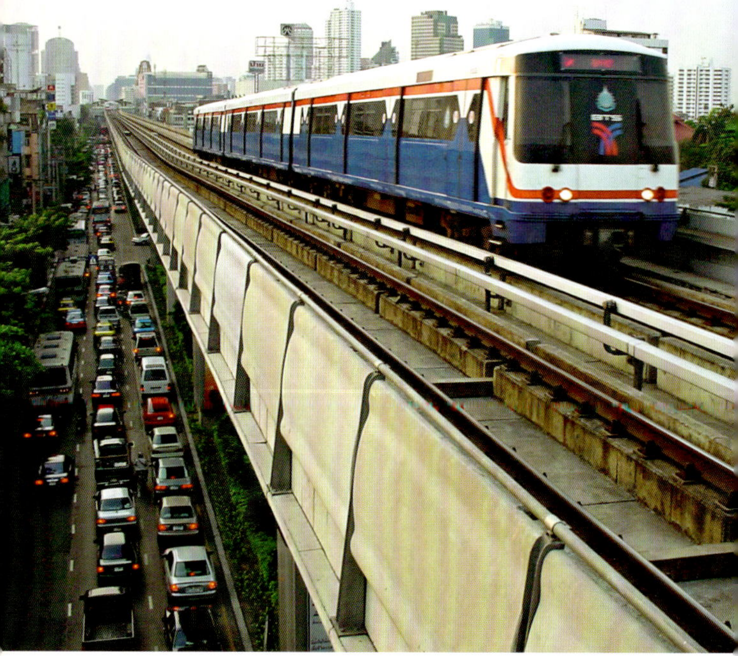
BTS

all other great cuisines of East and West; scores of glittering shopping plazas vie in their displays of the latest designer labels; luxurious city spas pamper the body like never before; kaleidoscopic nighttime entertainment attracts all preferences. . . . These and more make for a modern world of sheer delight.

Bangkok is a magical place — tolerant, funloving and imbued with a feeling of freedom. At times it may appear hectic. But what finally comes across is a good-natured acceptance of life with all its idiosyncrasies. Here, perhaps more than anywhere else in the world, the traveller can discover the unique amid the ease of the familiar.

14

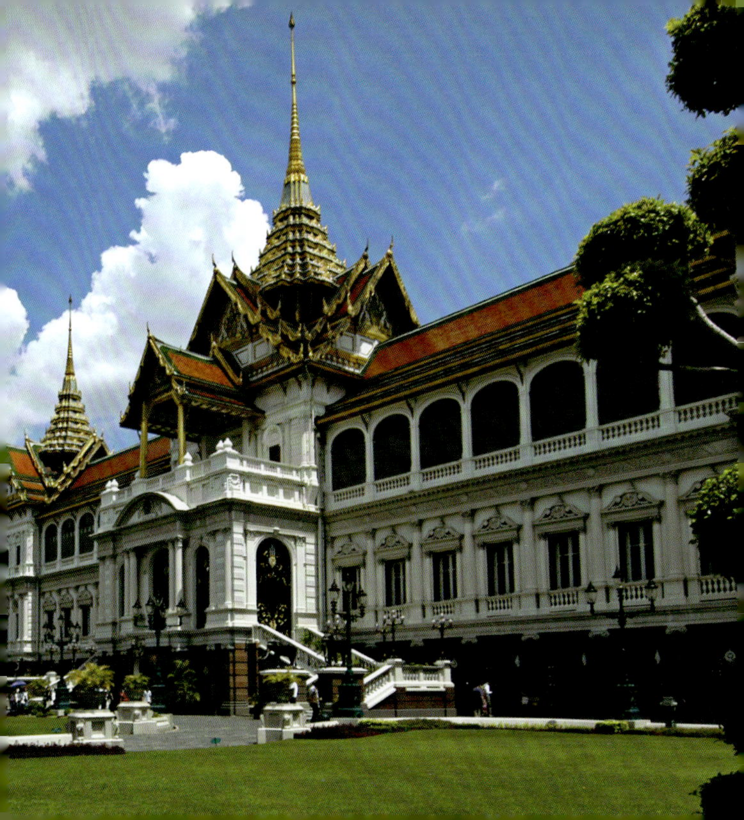

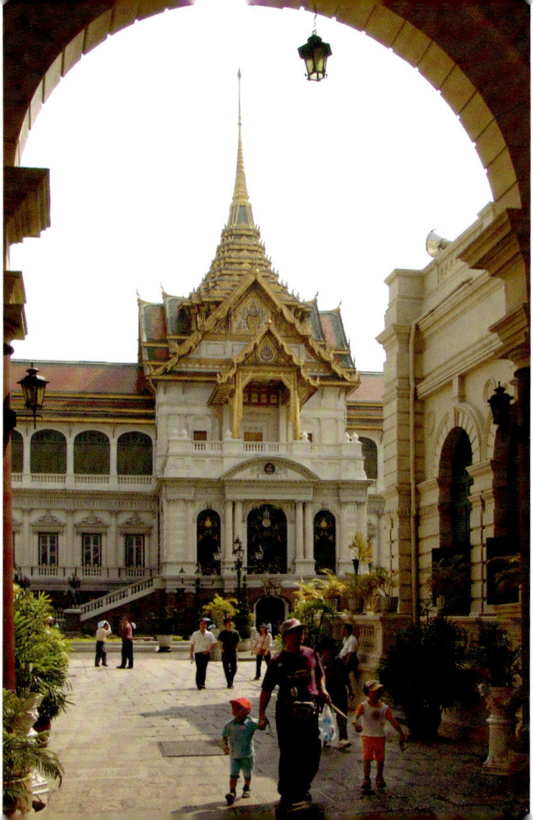

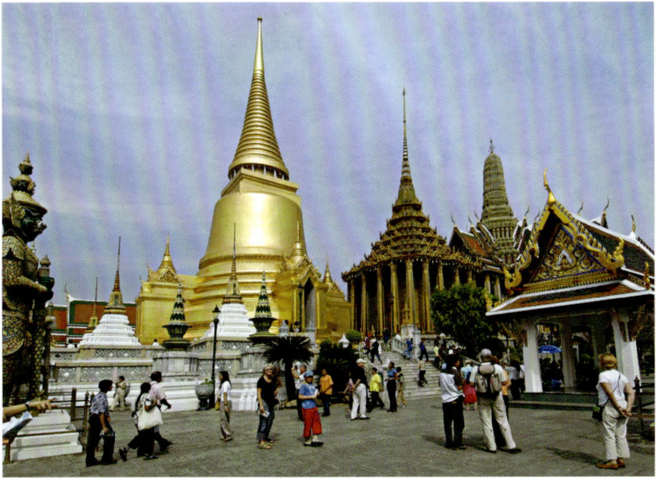

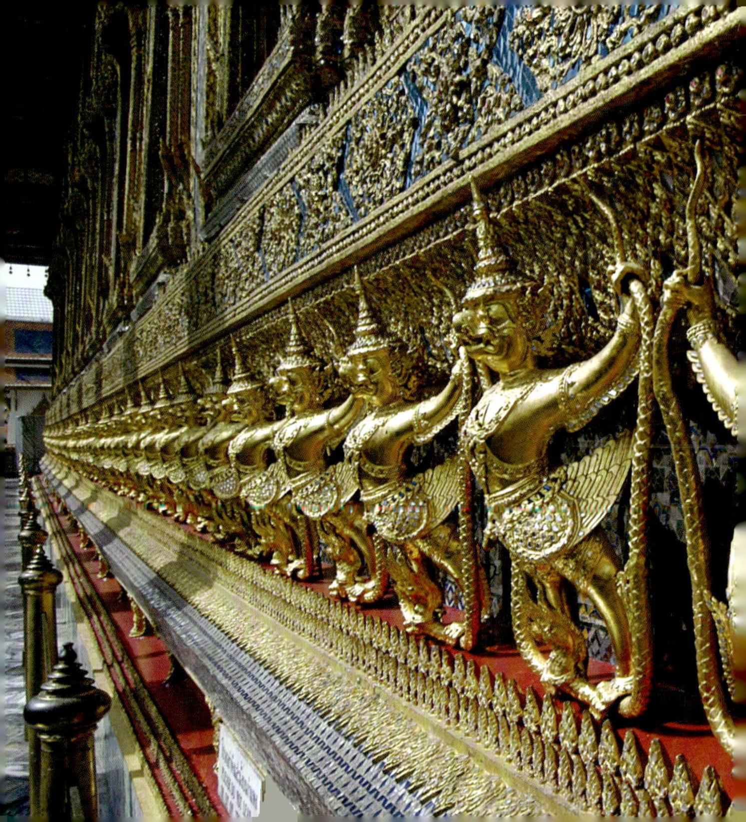

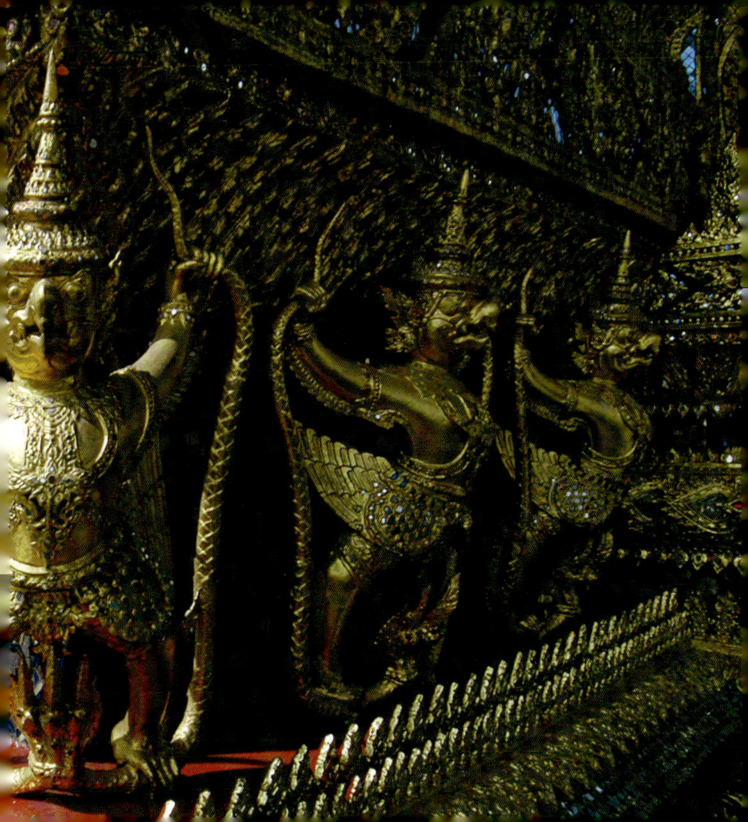

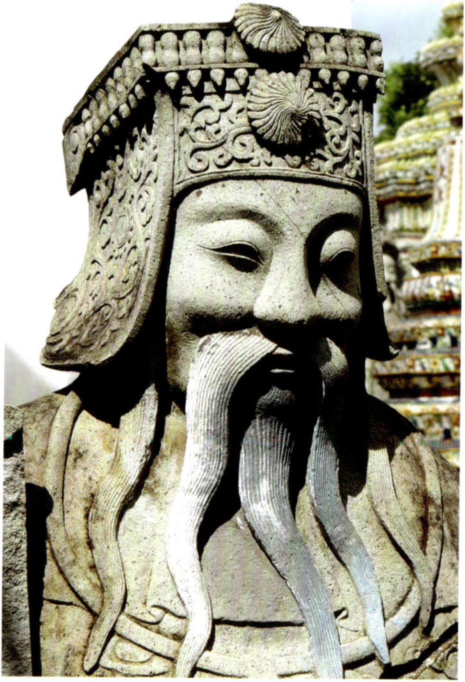

21

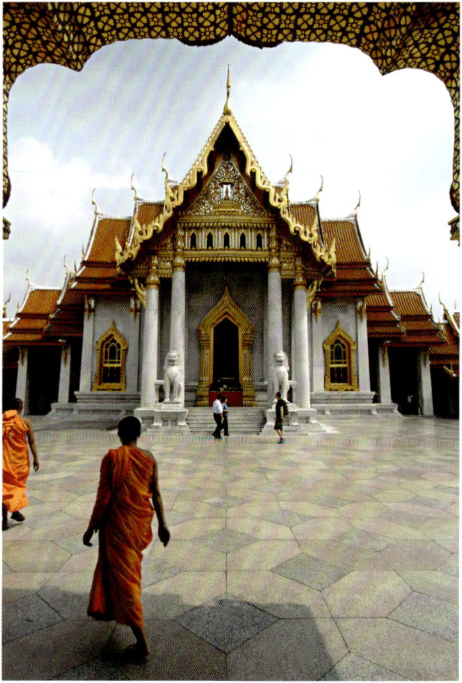

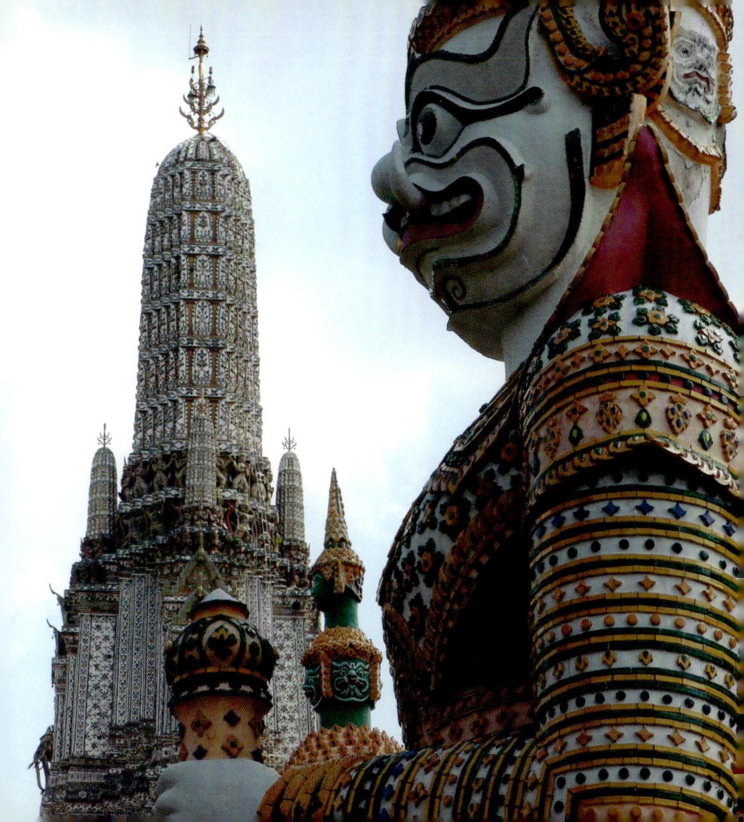

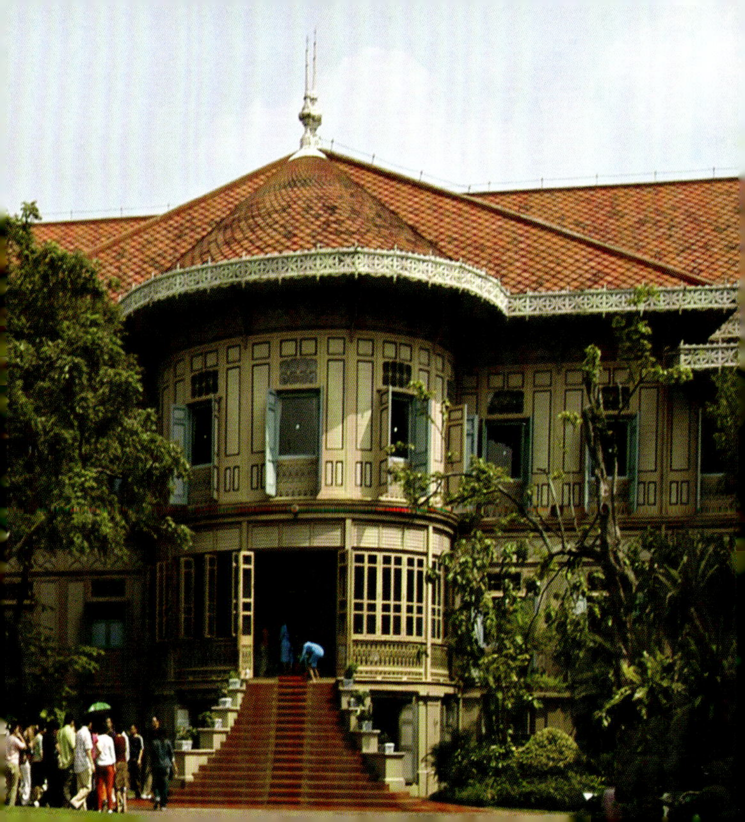

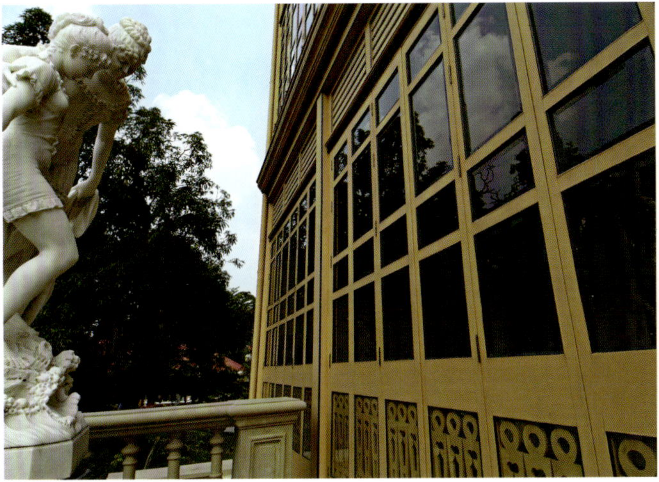

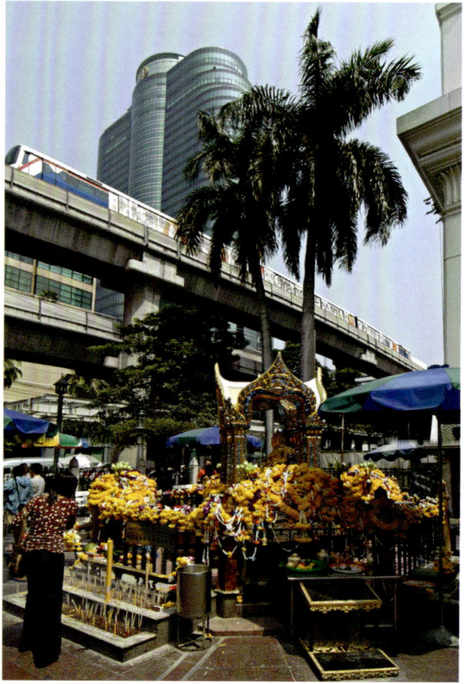

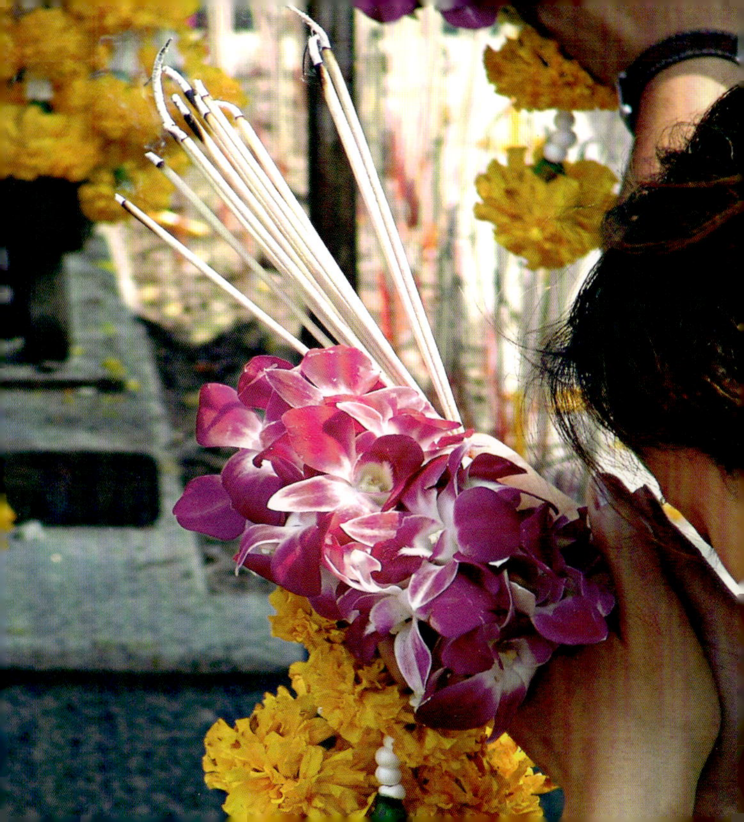

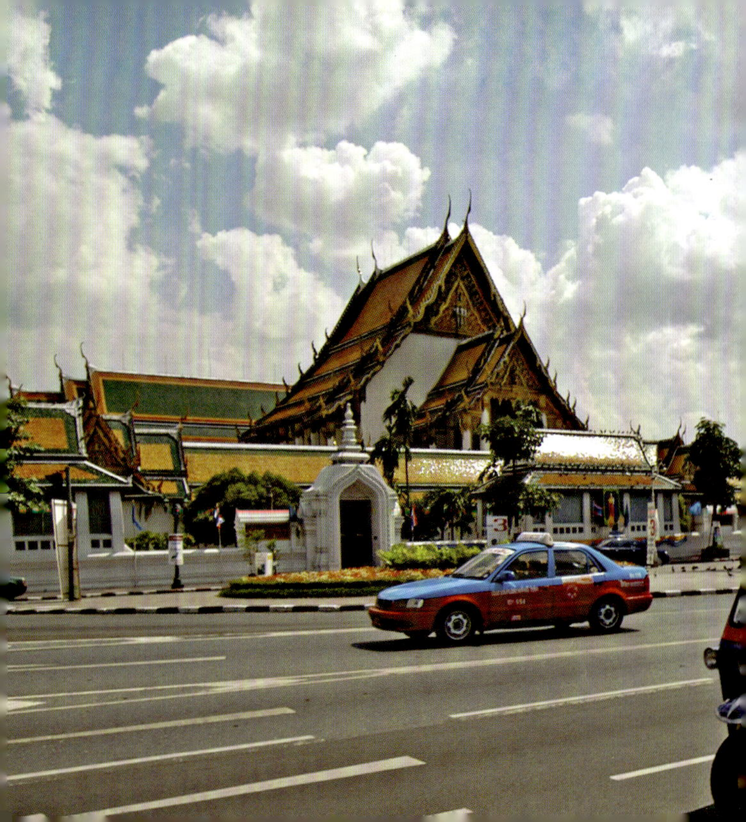

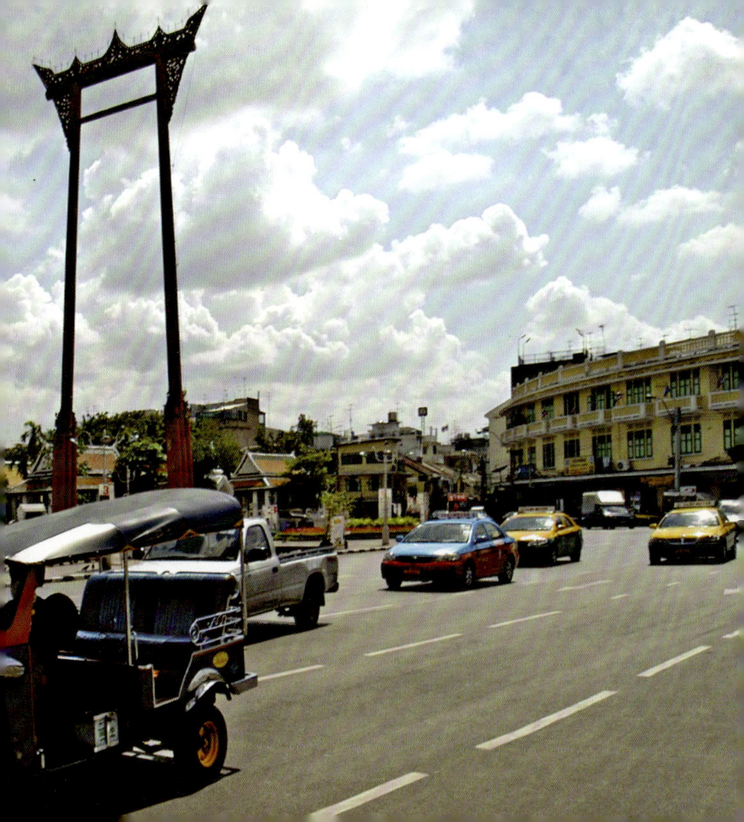

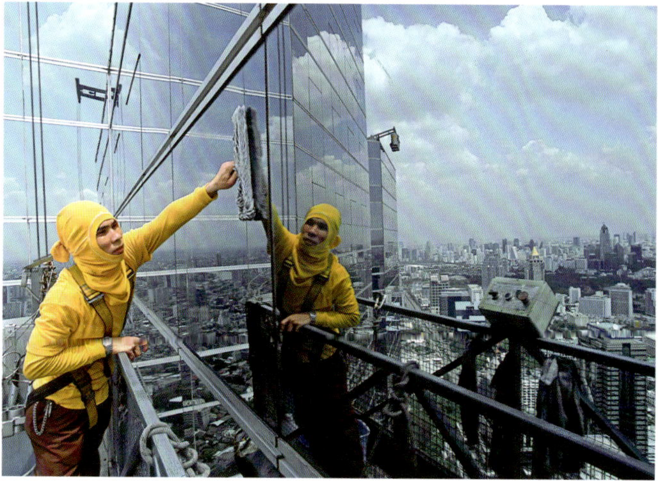

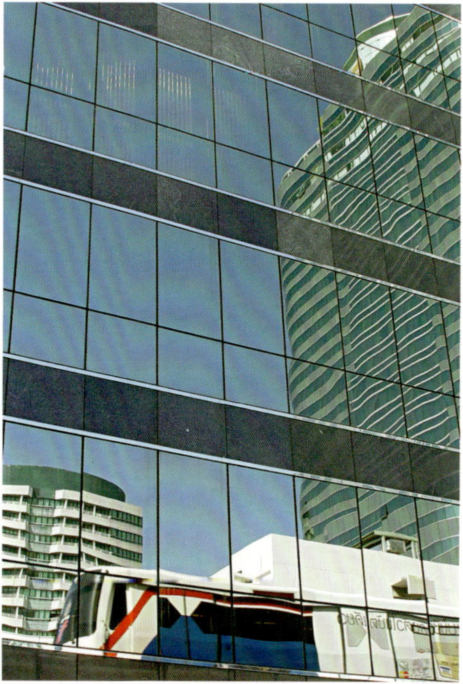

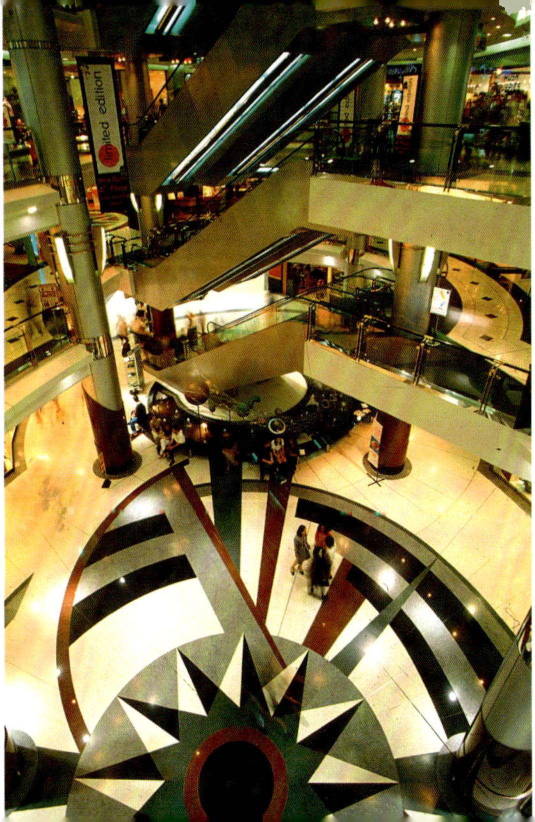
limited edition

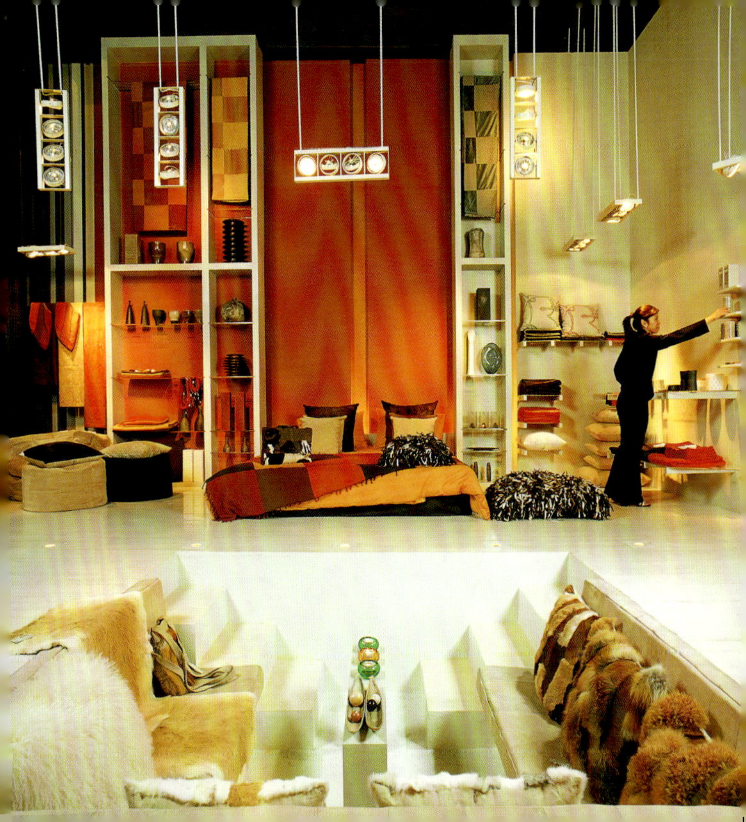

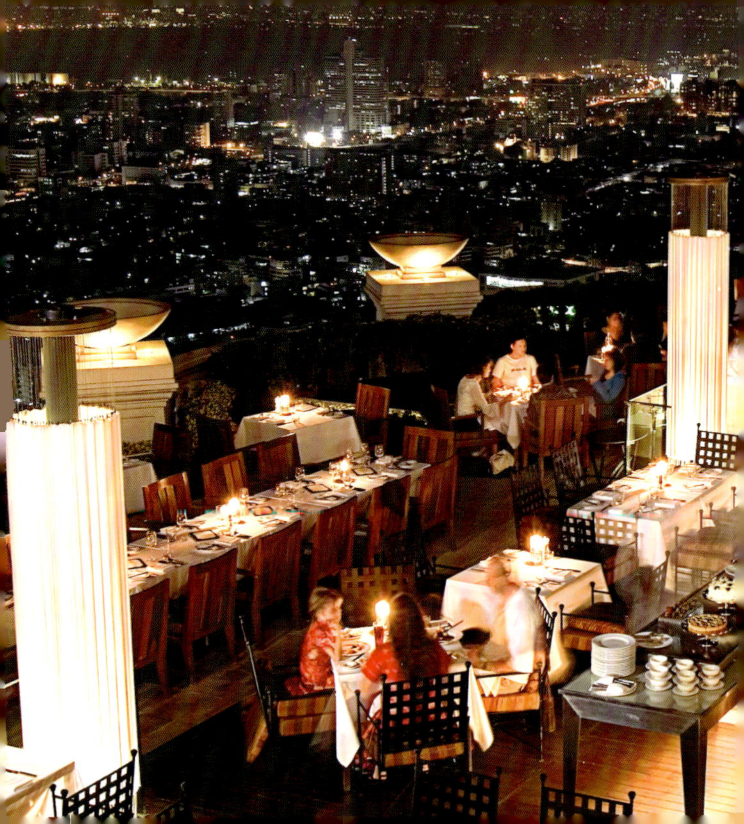

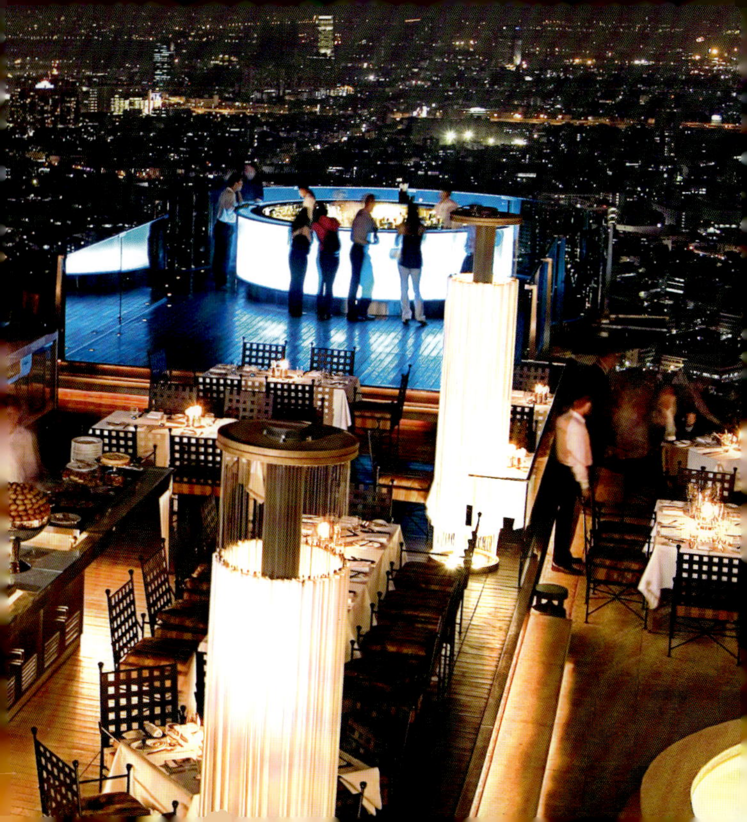

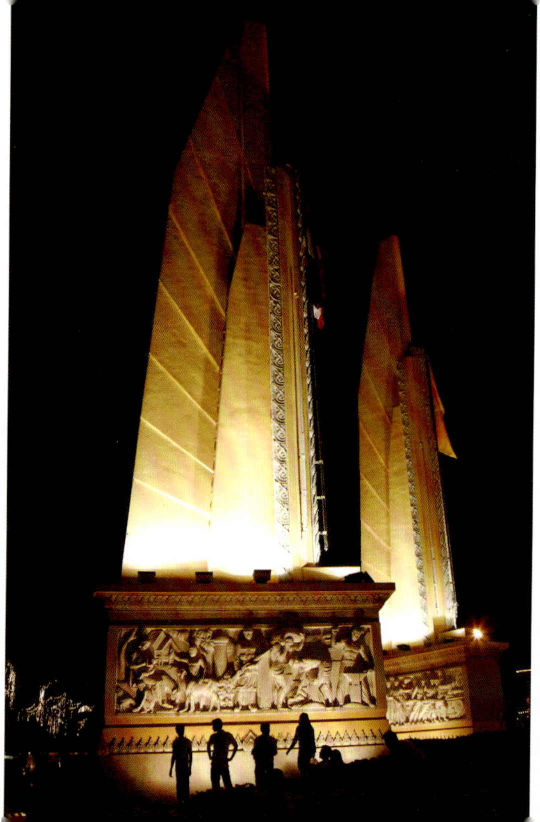

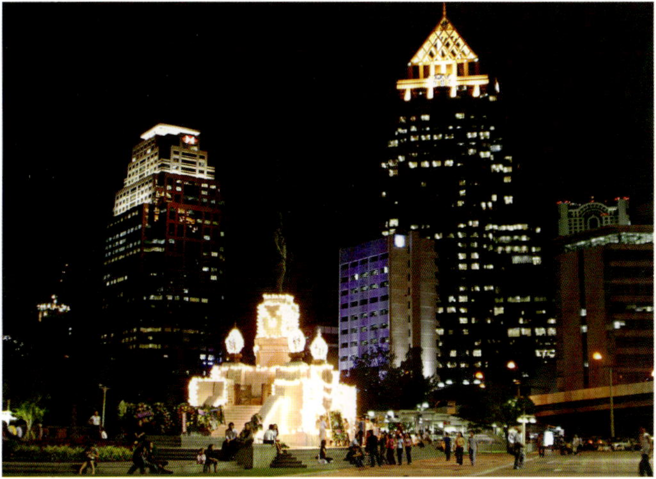

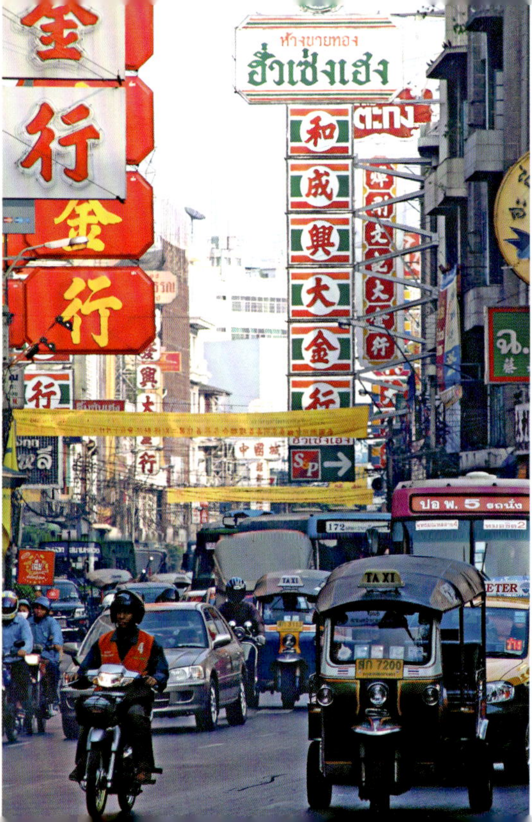
金
行
金
行
ห้างขายทอง
ฮั่วเซ่งเฮง
和
成
興
大
金
行
TAXI
TAXI

39

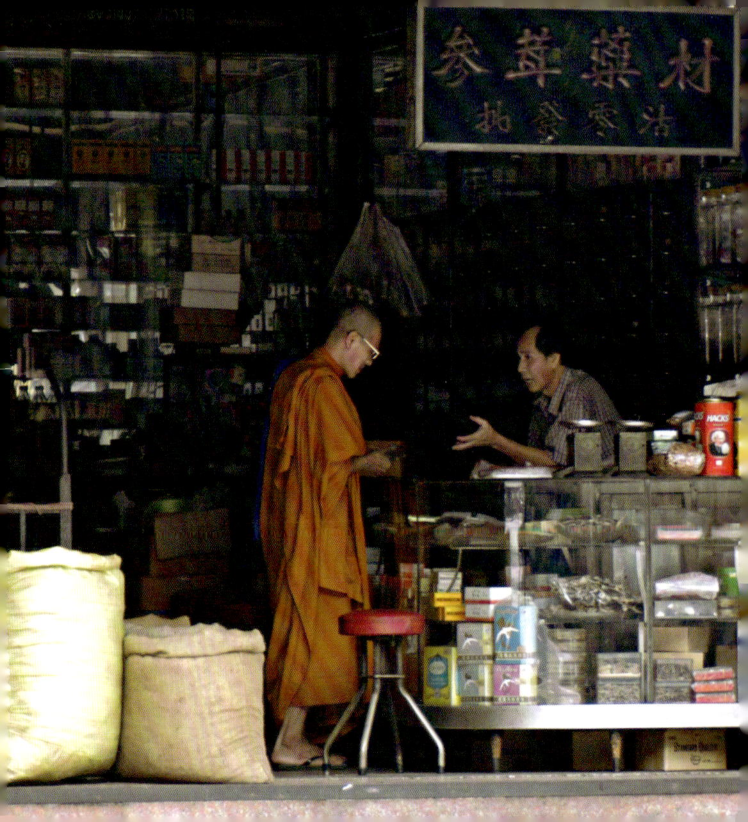
参茸藥材
批發零沽
HACKS

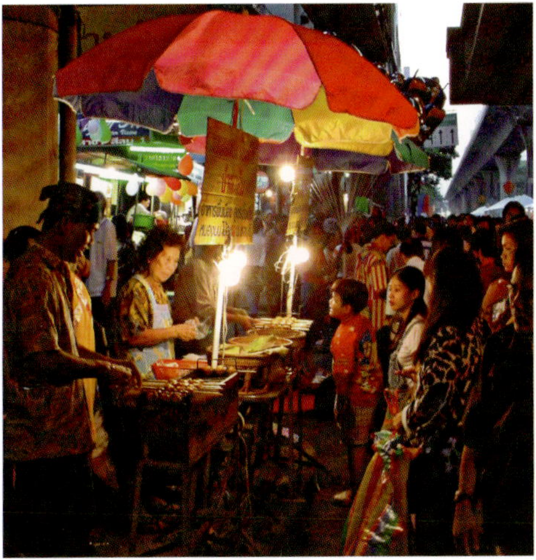

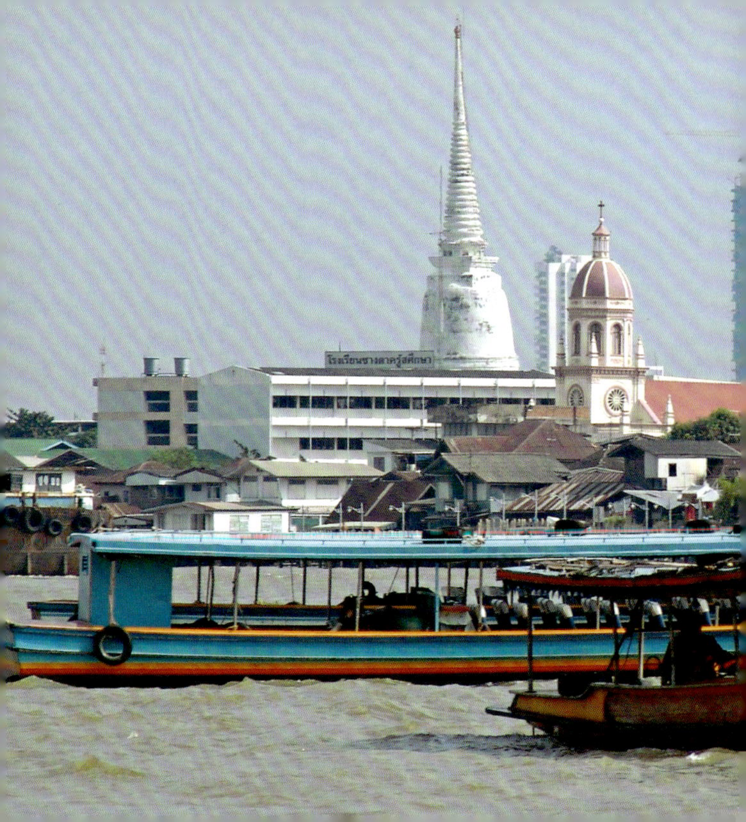
โรงเรียนซางตาครู้สศึกษา

WAT ARUN

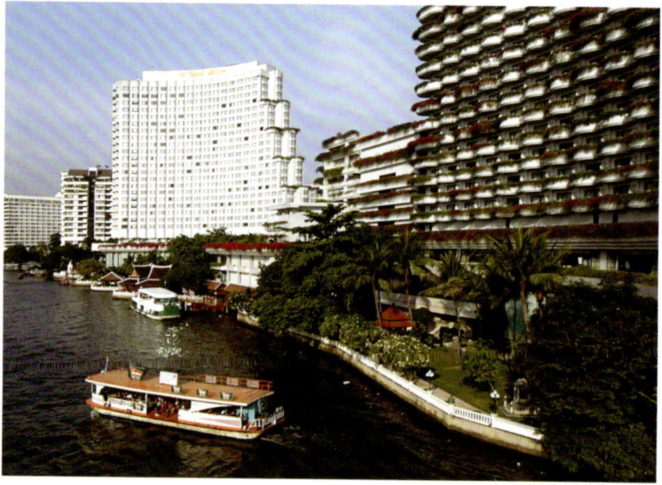

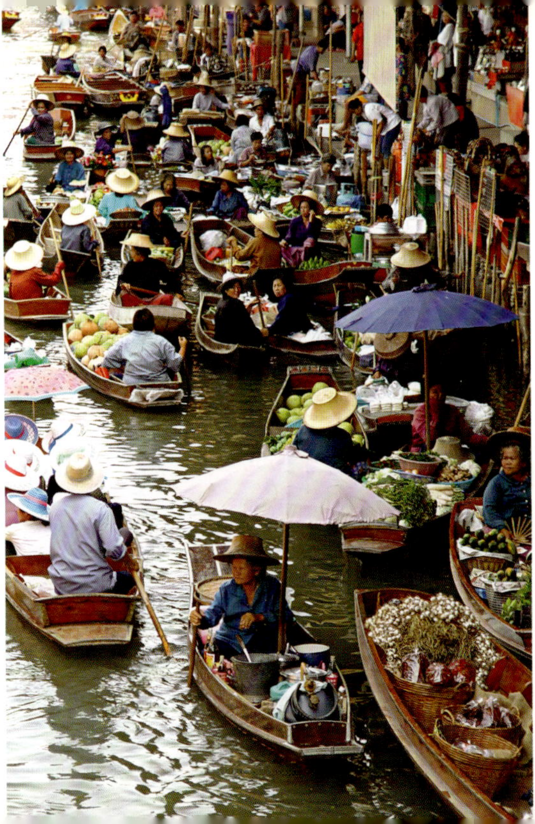

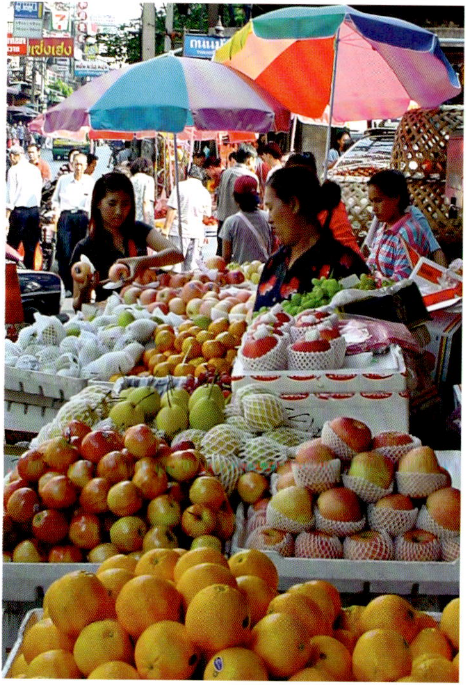

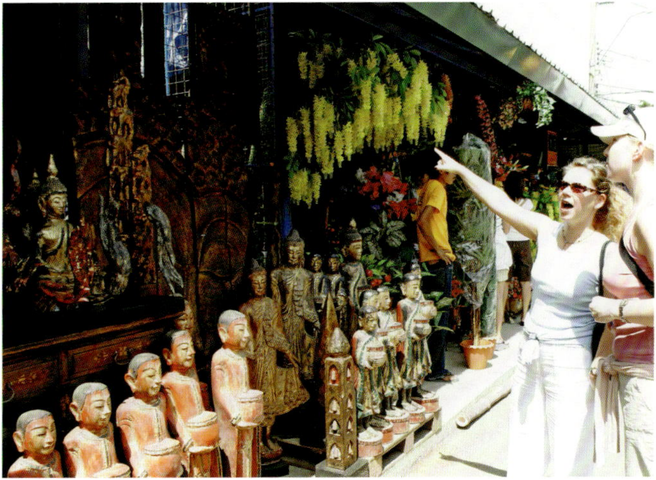

48

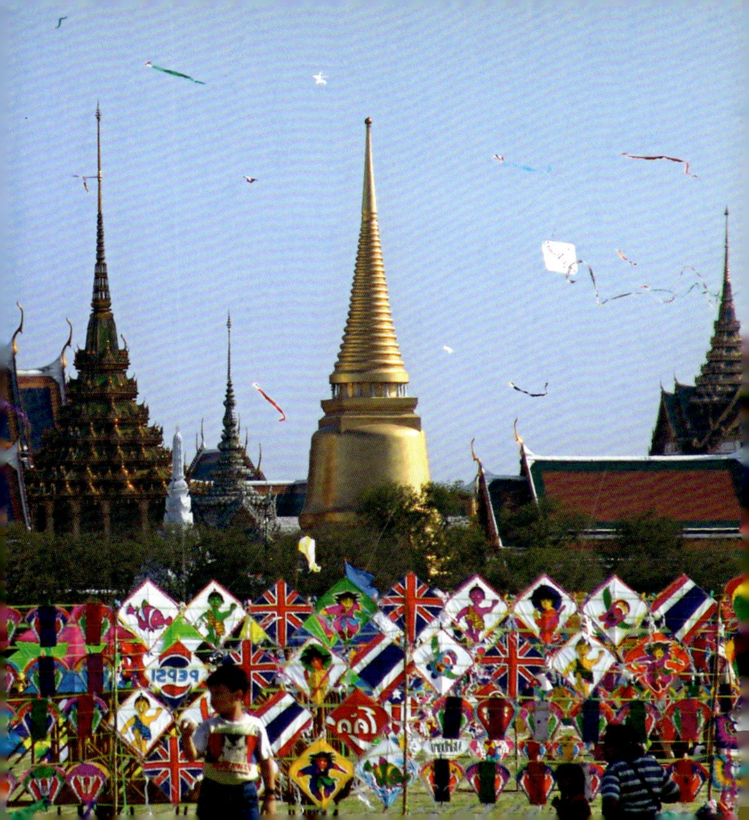

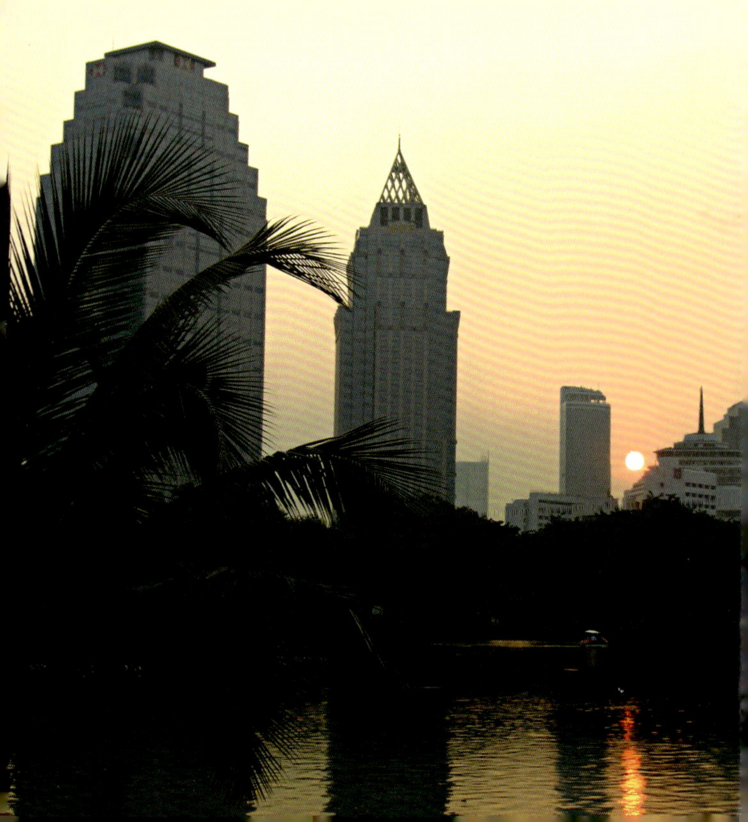

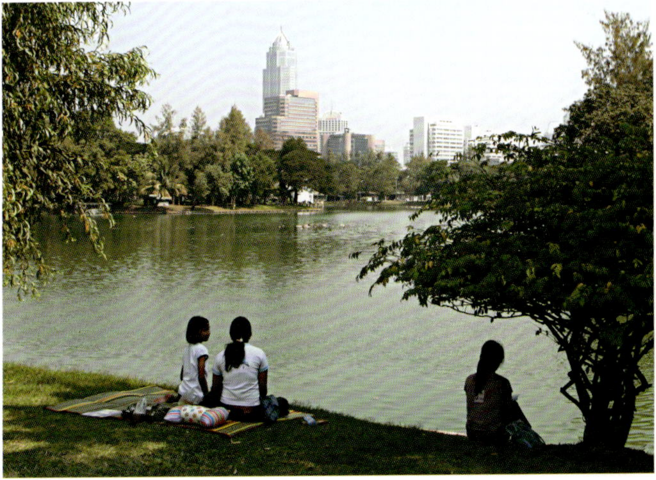

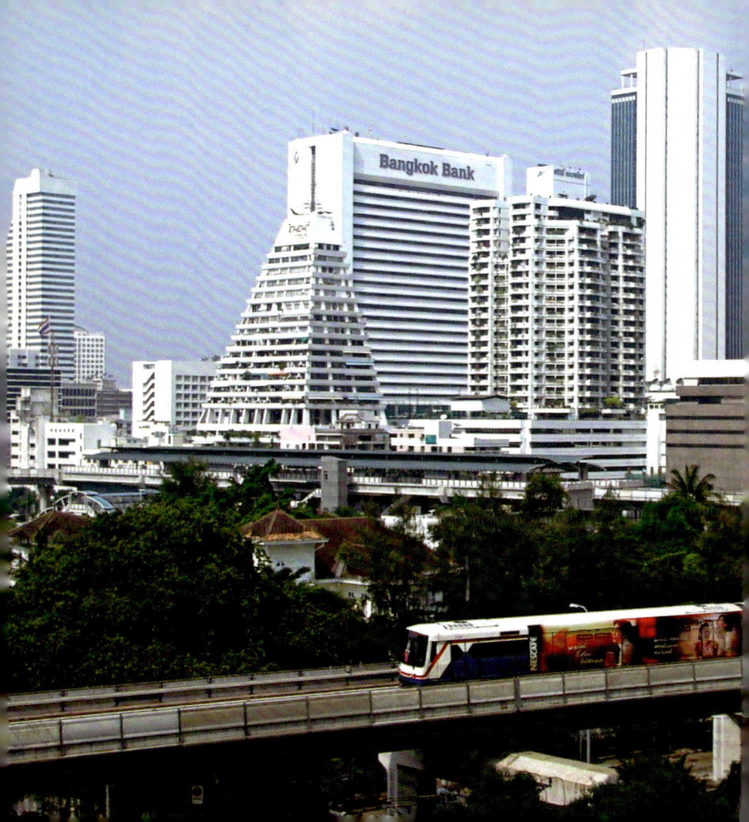
Bangkok Bank
NESCAFE

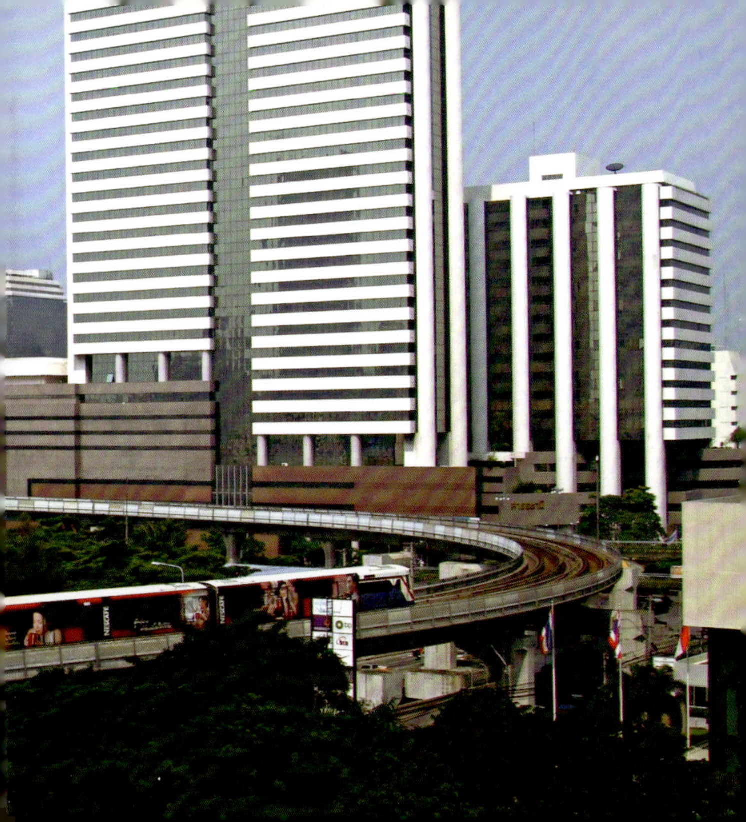

Cover: *At sunset, the Temple of Dawn glows beside the great Chao Phraya River.*

Pages 2–3: *Since the early 1980s, Bangkok has burgeoned into a modern high-rise metropolis.*

Page 4: *The Temple of the Emerald Buddha is located in the grounds of the Grand Palace.*

Page 6: *In Bangkok, even fast-food restaurant mascots greet you with a wai.*

Page 7: *The Chao Phraya, 'the River of Kings', flows through the heart of Bangkok.*

Page 8: *The Golden Mount with its temple was long the highest point in Bangkok.*

Page 9: *The Emerald Buddha is the most sacred image in the land.*

Page 10: *Saffron-robed monks are a familiar sight on the streets of Bangkok.*

Page 11: *Bangkok is a city of contrasts between the traditional and the modern.*

Page 12: *The 'skytrain' elevated railway system whisks you about town far above the traffic.*

Page 14: *Images of elephants are ubiquitous; there was a time when the elephant featured on the national flag.*

Pages 14–15: *The Grand Palace, formerly the king's residence, is now a must-see tourist attraction.*

Page 16: *The gateway to the once-forbidden Grand Palace is now open to all.*

Page 17: *The Temple of the Emerald Buddha is a magnificent array of shrines and spires.*

Pages 18–19: *On a chapel wall at the Temple of the Emerald Buddha guardian images glisten.*

Page 20: *A Chinese stone image stands guard at Wat Po, Bangkok's second most important temple.*

Page 21: *Wat Po is Bangkok's largest monastery.*

Page 22: *The Marble Temple is a superb melding of Thai and Italian architecture.*

Page 23: *At the Temple of Dawn, beside the Chao Phraya River, a fearsome guardian stands.*

Page 24: *Built around a century ago, Vimanmek Palace is the largest golden teak building in the world.*

Page 25: *Vimanmek Palace was built by King Rama V in the carefully planned Dusit district.*

Page 26: *The famous Erawan Shrine stands at the busy heart of downtown Bangkok.*

Page 27: Making a wish and saying a prayer at the Erawan Shrine are cherished customs.

Page 28–29: The tuk-tuk taxi and the Giant Swing are Bangkok icons.

Page 30: Hundreds of glass office towers keep window cleaners busy.

Page 31: In the modern city an office tower reflects a passing skytrain.

Page 32: Bangkok is replete with swish malls and stylish shopping.

Page 33: Shop till you drop amongst some of Asia's coolest designs.

Pages 34–35: Sirocco at the State Tower — upscale dining atop the city's second tallest building.

Page 36: Democracy Monument is the centrepiece of ceremonial Ratchadamnoen Avenue.

Page 37: At night, artfully lit, select business districts resemble Chicago or Tokyo.

Page 38: Chinatown, once the commercial heart of the city, still bustles with business today.

Page 39: Street food is hugely varied and highly affordable.

Page 40: Traditional Chinese shops still abound in old Chinatown.

Page 41: Wherever you go, well into the night, tasty snacks are cooked up in the street.

Page 42–43: An extraordinary range of vessels ply the mighty Chao Phraya River.

Page 44: Some of Bangkok's best hotels hug the riverside.

Page 45: Canal floating markets are traditions of Bangkok and the Central Plains.

Page 46: Fruitsellers line Charoen Krung Road in busy Chinatown.

Page 47: Everything from statues to sturgeons is on sale at Chatuchak Market.

Page 48: A nationalist kite-flyer at Sanam Luang, in the historical city centre.

Pages 48–49: Flying kites is a very popular pastime at Sanam Luang, not far from the Temple of the Emerald Buddha.

Page 50: Rising above beautiful Lumpini Park, prestigious office towers soar.

Page 51: Lumpini Park is the city centre's green lung and peaceful refuge.

Pages 52–53: A skytrain arcs through the downtown business district.

Page 56: At Wat Po there lies a colossal reclining Buddha, covered in gold leaf.

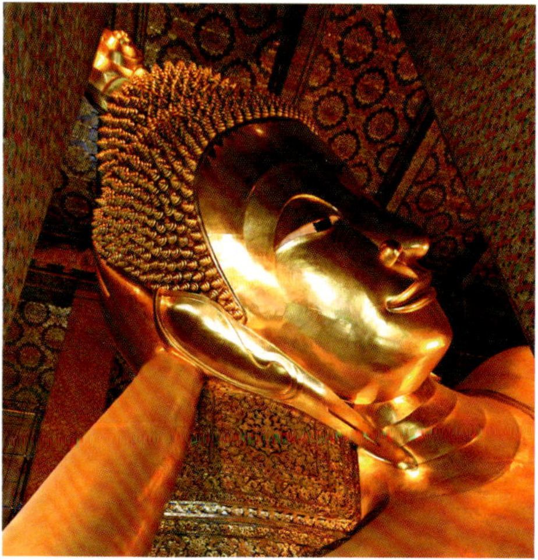

Acknowledgements

The publisher would like to thank the following whose assistance has made this book possible:

Thai Airways International Public Co. Ltd., Tourism Authority of Thailand, Sirocco Restaurant, Ramita Saisuwan, Keith Mundy and Keith Hardy.

Photo Credits

*The photographs in the book were taken by **Dave Lloyd** with the exception of the following:*

Leon Schadeberg: *30, 32, 34–35*

Nalinmard Sriphum: *11, 31*

Mark Standen: *33*

Authors

Dave Lloyd *is an Australian photographer based in Thailand, where his work has been widely exhibited. He has travelled extensively capturing on film sights, scenes and everyday life.*

John Hoskin *is an award-winning travel writer who has been based in Thailand since 1979. He is the author of more than 20 books on travel, art and culture in Southeast Asia.*